Women Stop the Chase

Let God's Man Find You

(Proverbs 18:22)

By

Dr. Mary M. Gillam, Col (Ret), USAF

Cover and photo by Create Space

For additional books by the Author and booking information:

- ❖ http://MaryMGillamLiteraryEnterpriseLLC.com
- ❖ Dr.MaryM.Gillam@gmail.com

Printed in the United States of America

Dedication

To Almighty God who gave me the vision and privilege to write this book so that it can inspire and motivate women to follow God's plan for relationships.

Acknowledgments

When I first contemplated writing this book, I discussed it with several male and female colleagues to get their perspective. I owe each of them a debt of gratitude for taking the time from their very busy schedules to listen to my book proposal and give me their honest assessment on the topic. Your thoughts and perceptions provided me with a wealth of information to ponder and consider.

I also want to thank my family members and Christian brothers and sisters for your continuous support and Godly counsel. You have inspired me beyond measure. Your insight and encouragement along this journey has been commendable. Thank you so much.

Finally, I want to thank everyone who will read this book. I pray that you will be blessed and that God will use you to be a blessing to others.

x

Table of Contents

Preface

Throughout society, there has been much debate on whether it is appropriate for a woman to chase or pursue a man in a relationship. There are arguments on both sides of the debate. Some people advocate that it is appropriate, while others postulate that we should return to traditional values of courtship. Cultural dynamics also contribute to how people perceive a woman's role in initiating a relationship.

As a Christian woman, I believe that God has a plan for our lives even when it comes to relationships. After spending time in prayer and in God's word studying this subject, I believe that there is no reason for a Christian woman to pursue or chase after a man. If that man is the one that God has for you, then he will want to take the role that God has ordained him to occupy. As a precious jewel in God's sight, you will be worth the pursuit. However, if he is unwilling to assume that role, then you are probably not the one that has his heart. Likewise, he is definitely not the one that God has for you.

God's pattern for relationships supersedes what society alludes to as acceptable behavior. As Christian women, if we are willing to trust God for our eternal salvation, then we must be willing to trust Him in every aspect of our lives. In addition, as holy women of God, we must adhere to His principles and set the example for others to follow. Therefore, if you desire to be married, let God bring the right mate into your life. If you are willing to wait, God will present you to the one that He has already identified for you.

Warmest Regards,

Mary
Mary Gillam

Introduction

> *"I alone know the plans I have for you, plans to bring you prosperity and not disaster, plans to bring about the future you hope for"* *(Jeremiah 29:11, GNT).*

Several years ago, I awoke one night from a deep sleep and literally heard the words, "Stop the chase. Let God's man find you." The words hit me like a brick. I knew what God was saying and I needed to surrender and obey. Little did I know that these words would forever change my perspective on relationships.

Although I grew up in a wonderful Christian home with my paternal grandmother, and knew that God had a plan and purpose for my life, I thought that I knew *better* when it came to finding my mate. Like so many ladies, I looked at superficial things. I will admit that I perhaps did not use sound wisdom. If I saw him from afar, I probably spent my time wondering, "If he was the one?" If he caught me looking, I would simply give him an innocent smile. Once he turned his head, I would resume the stare. How many times have we all been caught in this cat and mouse game? Can any of you ladies, identify with me? I promise, I want tell if you do.

Unfortunately, I also know how it feels to deem that he is the one—and yet he feels differently. During a conversation with one of my uncles several years ago, he indicated that the Lord had instructed him to tell me to guard my heart. I knew the significance of that word and could easily relate it to what was occurring in my life. What is interesting is on that particular day I had been reading the same passage of scripture that my uncle quoted to me.

"Keep thy heart with all diligence, for out of it are the issues of life" (Proverbs 4:23, KJV).

Regrettably, sometimes, people engage in relationships and they are ill-prepared. They go into the relationship looking for the other person to fulfill them. They enter the relationship broken and remain in that state. They never seem to understand why the relationship is in chaos. For years, they may go through the motion of being happy, never realizing that God has a better plan for their lives. As Christians, we must be willing to trust God.

Despite the fact that I was a college graduate and had a good job, I was missing the mark when it came to relationships. Something was not working and I needed to take time to find out why. For years, I withdrew from the dating circuit so that I could work on me. I needed to be honest with the Lord and myself. I refused to be bound by internal or external influencers that did not align with God's plan for me. Let me state for the record that although family and friends at times have your best interest at heart, you have to trust God. By conducting this self-introspection, it proved to be the best thing that I could have ever done.

I began seeking God with all of my heart. I knew that God loved me and only wanted the best for me. So, I asked, "Lord, what am I missing?" In my quest, I started reading and meditating on His word. The passage that God directed me to read was:

> *"He who finds a wife finds a good thing and obtains favor of the Lord" (Proverbs 18:22, NASB)*

Wow! It was like a light bulb went off in my head. Although I had read this passage many times, this was my moment of revelation. God has a divine plan for establishing relationships and I wanted to understand that plan.

Let me ask you, "Do you believe that God has a plan for each of our lives?" If your answer is yes, then do you believe that God's wisdom is what we should apply at each stage of our lives?" Yet, when it comes to relationships, why do we sometimes believe that we know best (or who is best for us)?

When we apply the wisdom of God in relationships, then we have to trust Him for the results. Proverbs 3:13-14 reminds us that *"Blessed are those who find wisdom, those who gain understanding, for she is more profitable than silver and yields better returns than gold"* (TNIV).

4

While on this journey to understand Proverbs 18:22, God began to reveal things to me regarding relationships which established the premise for this book. It was out of my own experiences that I began this search. There is a right way and God was ready to teach me as long as I was willing to learn. I believe that when we truly want God's will for our lives, He will make the vision plain.

In the following chapters, I will discuss what I have learned over the course of my pursuit to understand God's plan for relationships. Despite what society may advocate as the path toward successful relationships, I have chosen to use God's word as the roadmap.

Regardless of the bumps and bruises along the way, God's plan still produces a *win-win* situation. At the end of the day, one can never forget that there are human elements in the picture. Therefore, we have to do what we can and leave the rest to our Heavenly Father.

As you read this book, I pray that God will speak to your heart and that this book will be a blessing in your life. May the passages of scripture minister to you and the examples provide a witness of God's unwavering love. May you rest in the knowledge of knowing that God will meet your every need according to His riches in glory.

The Relationship Journey

Boaz asked, "Whose damsel is this" (Ruth 2:5, KJV)?

W e all know the story of Adam and Eve. When Adam was in the Garden of Eden, he was surrounded by animals. He was actively naming each species and taking care of them. However, in Genesis 2:20, we find that his heart longed for a mate. How do we know this? *"So the man gave names to all the livestock, the birds in the sky and all the wild animals but for Adam no suitable helper was found"* (Genesis 2:20, TNIV).

Since our Heavenly Father is omniscient or all-knowing, then He knew Adam's heart desire to have a companion. Therefore, God created Eve. Not only was Eve taken out of the rib of Adam, God presented her to Adam. What was the relationship pattern established here? As I pondered over this passage, I thought long and hard. I wanted to know what God intended me to learn from re-reading this scripture. As I remained open to God's direction, I learned several lessons along the way. The first lesson is depicted below:

Lesson #1

God knows who and what we need in our lives.

Since God's timing is the best timing, then He also knows when to bring that person into our lives. This statement reflects the second lesson that I learned. For example, Adam was busy taking care of the garden. When God saw that the timing was right, then He *provided* Eve to Adam. Do you believe that God's timing is the best timing? Before you answer, I invite you to take some time and ponder your response.

Lesson #2

Do not under estimate God's timing for doing things. He knows what is best.

In Proverbs 18:22, I found myself concentrating on the phrase, "He who *finds* a wife…" From a generic perspective, to find something primarily means that you are looking for that item. In this passage, the man is conducting the search. He has obviously decided to seek after the woman that he wants to develop a meaningful God-centered relationship. Hopefully, he has spent time seeking God, so now he is ready to begin seeking after you which provides the basis for lesson three.

Lesson #3

Let the man [of God] initiate the pursuit.
In essence, let him *find* you.

If you are the one that God has created for him, then his heart will cling to you. There will be a *heart connection* which leads to lesson four. He will want to pursue you—God's way. There have been times in my own life, when I failed to understand this process. I was determined to create something that was not there. Now, I can definitively proclaim, "God's way is the best way."

In Genesis 29:18, we find the story of Jacob and Rachel. The bible indicates that when Jacob saw Rachel, he *loved* her. Jacob recognized the one that made his heart rejoice. He had fallen in love with his soul mate. There were no mind games or puzzles to resolve. He knew that Rachel was the one for him. Of all the other women that Jacob could have loved, it was Rachel that stole his heart. Likewise, Rachel did not have to trick Jacob or buy him gifts to make him care for her. It occurred naturally. Unfortunately, there are some of us who never got the "memo." How many times have we been caught us in this scenario—buying presents in an attempt to win love?

If God brings couples together, then the relationship will be genuine. It did not matter how long

Jacob had to work for Rachel's hand (14 years to be exact), he was determined to make Rachel his wife. However, despite some challenging circumstances, Jacob prevailed.

Let's look at some of Jacob's challenges in his pursuit to win his bride. Laban, who was Rachel's father, had another daughter named Leah. According to biblical history, it was customary that the older daughter marry prior to the younger daughter. Unfortunately, Leah was still single. Laban now had a *problem*. He could not allow Jacob to marry Rachel until Leah was married. Laban, been the cunning man that he was, devised a plan. He would permit Jacob to marry his daughter—but initially which one? Uhm …

During the wedding ceremony, the bride's face was concealed. Can you imagine Jacob's excitement? He had worked seven years for his bride. His heart was probably pounding out of his chest. I can imagine him saying, "I am going to finally get the love of my life."

Unfortunately, Jacob would be in for the surprise of his life. As Gomer Pyle use to say on the Andy Griffith show, "Surprise…surprise." It was not until the wedding night that Jacob realized he had been betrayed.

Although Jacob thought he had married Rachel, it was really Leah. Wow! Hollywood has nothing on this story. Jacob is at his lowest, so he can only go up from here.

Laban had executed the perfect deception. As students of the bible, we know that Jacob with the assistance of his mother had carried out a major deception on his brother Esau years earlier. Some people may think that this was the perfect *pay-back*. Since Laban was also Jacob's uncle, it appears that deception ran in their family. Jacob was furious with Laban. I envision that he may have asked, "How could you have done such a thing?"

Yet, Jacob still loved Rachel. The heart connection between Jacob and Rachel was not imaginable, but was authentic. During that timeframe, multiple marriages were permitted.   Therefore, Jacob continued to pursue Rachel and worked another seven years for her hand in marriage. For Jacob, this was part of God's plan for his life. Therefore, he was willing to surrender and obey.

Another example of establishing a heart connection is found in the book of Esther. We all know the story in which King Ahasuerus was looking for a new queen to replace Vashti. From a comical perspective, some may say, Vashti had a bad hair day or a headache and did not want any part of the king's antics. When asked to dance before the king's guests at the party, the queen refused. This was unacceptable behavior. Since Vashti refused to dance for the king, she was removed from her position as queen.

According to Esther 2:2, the king's servants began the search for Vashti's replacement. Many of the young ladies were selected to go before the king. Yet, it was Esther who *stole* the king's heart. *"So Esther was taken unto King Ahasuerus into his house…and the king loved Esther above all the women, and she obtained grace and favor in his sight…"* (Esther 2:16-17, KJV).

Esther was later made the queen. It is amazing how God orchestrated this relationship. Vashti had to be removed before Esther could assume her new position. Based on things that were occurring behind the scenes, Esther had to be in position to be able to later help her fellow countrymen. Unless Esther was made queen, this would not have occurred.

Some of you may be wondering, "What about Ruth and Boaz?" If the man should pursue the woman, then how do you explain Ruth's actions? Ruth was instructed by Naomi (her mother-in-law) to go to a gathering in which Boaz would be in attendance. This could be interpreted as pursuing him. This entire episode is described in Ruth 3:1-9.

Yet, after reading the entire book of Ruth, what I found was that Boaz had already set his affection toward Ruth in an earlier chapter. When he returned from Bethlehem, Boaz inquired about Ruth. He noticed her "working" in the field. He asked, *"Whose damsel is this"* (Ruth 2:5, KJV)? The complete story is described in Ruth 2:5-16. I would speculate that if Boaz had not been interested in Ruth, he probably would not have asked about her identity. However, based on the reading, he was definitely interested in her.

Ruth was an interesting woman. Her husband had previously died. Although she could have returned to her family, she chose to go with her mother-in-law. Since accompanying Naomi back to her home country, Ruth was busy working in the field. She was not sitting idle. Little did Ruth know—she was making herself *discoverable* to her future mate. She had already caught the eye of Boaz. The pursuit was now in full motion.

The bible states that Boaz went through a series of events with his fellow countrymen in order to make Ruth his bride. Boaz had found his *help-mate* in Ruth and was willing to pursue her. It was apparent that Ruth cared for Boaz as well. One could assume that there was definitely a heart connection between Boaz and Ruth. God had already positioned them to eventually meet each other, which they did. Therefore, as the old cliché goes, "…and the rest is history."

If there is a heart connection between you and the one that God has [for you], then let God's man initiate the pursuit. If you are both praying to the [same] God asking Him to fulfill your desire for a mate, then, trust in God for the answer. Let God put His choice in your heart. It is unwise to begin claiming someone that was never yours in the first place. This is how many people get their hearts broken.

As Christians, let's stop putting limits on God. He has already given us the Holy Spirit to lead and guide us into all truth. He will enable us to make the right decisions. From the examples given above, we can see that God is more than capable of bringing the right people together. Since we were all designed to fulfill His master plan, then we know that God's plan is the ultimate way forward.

After reading this chapter, let me ask you to take some time and ponder the questions below:

1. Do you believe that God knows who and what you need in your life?
2. Do you believe that God's timing is truly the best timing?
3. Are you willing to let God's man pursue you?
4. Are you willing to let God create the heart connection between you and the one He has for you?

So, what do you *really* believe? Are you standing firm on those beliefs? Spend some time contemplating your answers and write them down. If you find yourself having to really think about your answers, then I encourage you to pray that God's will be done in every aspect of your life.

The purpose of this chapter was to share with you some lessons learned during my quest to understand God's plan for relationships. After writing this chapter, I believe that God had specific lessons that he wanted me to ascertain from this writing. In summary, the lessons are:

- ❖ God knows who and what we need in our lives.
- ❖ Do not under estimate God's timing for doing things.
- ❖ Let the man [of God] initiate the pursuit. In essence, let him *find* you.
- ❖ Let God create the heart connection between you and your potential mate. Don't try to create something that was never meant to be.

In addition to the lessons learned, we explored some biblical examples that were used to reiterate the lessons. Afterwards, I proposed several questions for you to ponder.

The next chapter will essentially challenge all of us to examine the degree in which we are trusting God.

Trusting God with the Decision

"Trust in the Lord with all thine heart and lean not unto thine own understanding. In all thy ways acknowledge Him and He shall direct thy paths" (Proverbs 3:5-6, KJV).

What does it mean to place your trust, confidence, faith, and hope in someone? The ultimate expectation is that they will not deceive you but are worthy of your trust. Despite this positive affirmation, there are times when we have all been betrayed. We have gone through the pain and suffered the hurt. Yet, there is one who will never betray our love or our trust. God loves us more than we could ever imagine. His word declares that we are to trust in Him completely.

As I continued to study God's word regarding relationships, He reiterated to me the importance of trust. He who created the universe is more than able to create the "right" relationships. Sometimes, we say that we are trusting in God, yet our actions fail to align with the trust. We will pray with our heart and begin to reason with our mind—so the battle begins. There are times when we become frustrated with waiting on God, and choose to make something happen that He never intended. Even when we know God's word and have received Godly counsel, we can still make unwise choices. Afterwards, with tears in our eyes, we look to heaven and ask, "Lord, how could this have ever happened to me?" How do I know? I've been there.

As I prayed over this book, the Lord revealed to me that there are women who have been hurt by relationships that He never intended for them. Yet, they decided to proceed forward. Having been one of those women in the past, I thought I knew what was best for me. I was independent and I made my own decisions. After suffering through some painful heart-breaks, I am convinced that God's plan is the best plan. In the natural, we can only see with our natural eyes, but God sees and knows everything to include who is "right" for us. We can trust in Him to help us to make the right decision. I believe that if we delight ourselves in Him, God will give us our heart's desire. He will bring the right person into our life. Therefore, as Christian women, we do not have to go on the prowl and begin to chase or pursue any man. We have to let God—be God.

Why am I passionate about this topic? Some people may think that adhering to Godly principles regarding relationships is "old-fashioned" and illogical. Teaching young girls to take pride in themselves and value what God has given them is our responsibility. As Christians, we have to understand God's word and how to apply it to our daily lives.

However, when we conduct our affairs just like the secular community, then we are no different. The bible states that we are the "salt of the earth." We are a peculiar people. We are to uplift the name of Christ. People should be able to distinguish us from the world. Our beliefs should be based on what God has written in His word.

Basically, as Christian women, we should not be pursuing after a man. When it comes to relationships, there is a role that men and women play. We need to understand those roles and whether we accept God's word as the ultimate guidelines. This is significant because we need to know what we believe. If you are questioned by a non-believer, then you need to have a firm foundation to base your belief.

Society has a multitude of differing viewpoints when it comes to relationships. Some of my colleagues and I had extended discussions on this issue. Although we respected each other's opinion, we stood firm in our beliefs.

During the research for this book, I conducted an anonymous survey across the United States with 100 participants. The purpose of the survey was to explore the perceptions of individuals concerning women initiating relationships with men. Of the 100 surveys distributed, 99 were returned generating a very favorable response return rate. Of the survey's 99 respondents, 52 (52.5%) were men while 47 (47.5%) were women. The age group ranged from 18 to 64.

Survey participants were asked, "If a man is really interested in dating a woman, should he be the one to initiate the contact?" The results were: 78 (78.8%) said yes, 10 (10.1%) selected no and 11 (11.1%) chose other. Five of the respondents who selected other indicated that the man should initiate the contact if he is interested. The remaining six respondents who chose other stated that either could initiate the contact. Figure 1 below depicts the results.

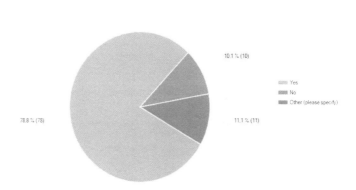

If a man is really interested in dating a woman, should he be the one to initiate the contact?

10.1 % (10)

Yes
No
Other (please specify)

78.8 % (78)

11.1 % (11)

Figure 1: Men Initiating Relationships with Women

Survey participants were also asked, "Should a woman pursue a man in a relationship?" The results are: 70 (70.7%) selected yes, 17 (17.2%) chose no, and 12 (12.1%) designated other. For the respondents who chose other, the unanimous answer was either individual can initate the relationship. However, one respondent did state, "It depends on the type of woman she is." Figure 2 displays the results.

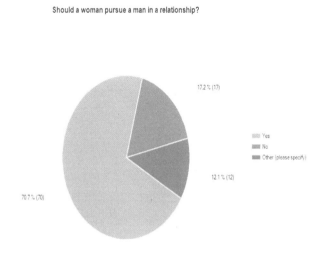

Should a woman pursue a man in a relationship?

17.2 % (17)

Yes
No
Other (please specify)

12.1 % (12)

70.7 % (70)

Figure 2: Women Initiating Relationships With Men

The final question that the respondents were asked was, "Would you encourage your daughter to pursue a man in a relationship?" The results were: 70

(70.7%) said yes, 17 (17.2%) selected no, and 12 (12.1%) chose other. Of the respondents who chose other, the primary theme was that it depended on the man and whether he was worth pursuing. However, one respondent stated, "Do as I say, not as I do." Another comment that I found extremely interesting was, "I would tell her to let herself be available in the sense that she lets him know she is looking for a relationship, but wait for him to initiate the actual relationship." Figure 3 depicts the results.

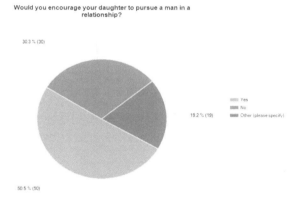

Figure 3: Advice for Your Daughter

The survey results yielded some interesting data. After reviewing the results, I wanted to compare several of the questions to see if age impacted the participants' response. Since the responses were evenly matched, there was no significant different between the age groups and their responses.

The survey was issued to a diverse audience. When asked if they thought if a man should initiate the relationship, the majority voted yes. However,when asked if a woman should initiate the relationship, the majority of the respondents also voted yes. These responses did not really generate any keen insight because they were basically equal. In addition, the majority of the respondents indicated that they would encourage their daugther to pursue a man.

Although this was an informal survey issued to a small sampling of people, the data presents some interesting dynamics for Christians. It reveals the perceptions and thought patterns of some individuals in our society today. Eventhough there are many factors influencing one's thought process, the word of God has to be the standard in which we as Christians base our decisions in life. I purposely chose to make the survey as broad as possible so that I could ascertain as many viewpoints as possible. From a personal perspective, I thought that the survey respondents would have responded differently when the "daughter dynamic" was added to the mix. Based on the results, the majority of the participants did not see anything egregious with encouraging their daughter to pursue a relationship with a man.

As Christian women we have to stand firm on God's word. Although we might sometimes be tempted to follow society's strategies for selecting a mate, God forbid. We have to be women of integrity, honor, and depict holiness. Whatever you are believing God for, just continue to press forward and trust that He will answer you in due season.

The focus of this chapter was trusting God with our life decisions. There is an adage that says, "Ways and actions speak louder than words." I wonder what our ways and actions are saying about each of us when it comes to trusting God.

This chapter also presented the results of an informal survey that described how some in society view the initiation of men and women relationships. In sum, there are many who believe that it is acceptable practice for women to pursue men in relationships. But, as Christian women, we must adhere to God's pattern for relationships. We can trust in Him with the final decision. We cannot allow society to alter our trust in God when it comes to selecting a mate. We can make a difference in society by being the Christian example that God would have us to be.

The next chapter addresses our willingness to press into the things of God. If you really want God to provide you with a mate, are you petitioning Him with that request? Are you pressing into the things that God has already promised His children?

Pressing into the Things of God

> *"I press toward the mark for the prize of the high calling of God in Christ Jesus"*
> *(Philippians 3:14, KJV).*

What do you want from God? If you are going to get anything from God, you are going to have to press your way into what God has for you. What does it mean to press? Webster defines it as "to act on with steady force or weight, to be insistent about, or to exert pressure." The word press could also mean to pursue with all diligence. For those of you who enjoy basketball, when the coach instructs you to go to a full court press, the game has now got serious.

As a Christian, that is how it is with God. You need to pursue what God has for you with everything that you have. Spending time in prayer and fasting is expected when you are placing a demand on the things of God. In other words, a press of any kind requires action. How determined are you to receive from God?

In Philippians 3:14, Paul describes himself using the analogy of a runner. He is exerting every effort toward the goal for the high calling of God in Christ Jesus. Like Paul's race, there is also a race designed for each and every one of us. God has charted the course and only you can run the race.

By pressing forward into the things of God, you will be able to win your race. God did not choose you based on your ability, your intellect, or on anything you can do in the natural. He planned from the beginning to empower you with His ability to do the job, which He as prepared for you. It is in the weakness of your natural ability that God displays His strength.

If you want to lay hold of the authority of God and walk in the supernatural, you can't do it from the couch. You have to press your way into the things of God. It is easy to stand at the edge of the sea, but it takes faith to launch out into the deep. If you want more power—press. If you want more wisdom—press. If you want more joy, then press your way into what God has for you! Therefore, if you want God to provide you with a mate, then by all means—press. Don't give up, but allow God to prove His faithfulness to you.

As Christian women, we can learn a lot from Olympic athletes. They display determination, diligence, and commitment toward their sport. Athletes train relentlessly. Rain or shine, they are at their training venues preparing themselves for the big prize. On the day of the event, they pop out of their starting blocks determined to finish the course. Regardless of how exhausted they might become, they continue to press toward the finish line. Let me ask you a simple question. How committed are you to your spiritual race? Are you as committed as the athlete to his natural race?

This is the kind of determination it takes to be a winner in the Kingdom of God. Not just physically, but spiritually. In Matthew 11:12, Jesus said, *"And from the days of John the Baptist, until now, the Kingdom of Heaven suffered violence, and the violent take it by force"* (KJV). When Jesus said these words, He wasn't just talking about going to heaven. He was talking about taking hold of the Kingdom of God in this earth. We need to possess the promised blessings of God such as healing, prosperity, love, joy, and peace. We can have kingdom blessings today. God wants to bless us. We have to be prepared to receive what He has for us.

In Genesis 32:26, Jacob wrestled with the angel in the wilderness. Jacob said, *"I will not let thee go, except thou bless me"* (KJV). We need to be determined to receive from God. Don't let go of God's promises to you. We may change, but God doesn't change. If he promised it, then He will do it. The bible declares that God is faithful.

I am reminded of the woman with the issue of blood as recorded in Luke 8:43-48. We are all familiar with this story. The lady was plagued with an issue of blood for 12 years. She went to numerous physicians with her problem, but to no avail. Then she heard that Jesus was in town. Now the press begins. Despite what people may have said to dissuade her from reaching Jesus, she was not to be deterred. I am certain that there were probably crowd police in the audience. Yet, if she had to go through persecution, ridicule, etc., she was not giving up. Just imagine her pushing through the emotional and physical baggage of 12 years to get to Jesus.

What baggage is stopping you from getting what God's has for you? This woman was determined to get her blessing. She knew that her only hope was in Jesus. With each step she took toward Jesus, I believe that she was exhibiting a true measure of faith. If I was to describe the tenants of faith as it pertained to this woman, they would look like this:

- F = *firm* in her commitment
- A = *acted* on her need
- I = *initiated* the road to healing
- T = *tenacious* with her desire
- H = *healthy* and whole

No conversation took place, but when she reached out to touch the hem of Jesus' garment, there was an exchange of healing for her faith. Jesus asked, *"Who touched me?"* (Luke 8:45, KJV). The disciples that were with Jesus were amazed that He would ask this question. There were a multitude of people surrounding Jesus—yet, one person truly touched Him. The bible indicates that virtue flowed out of Jesus at that very instance. Jesus was touched by this woman's infirmity. The physical touch was only symbolic of the spiritual touch. By faith, the woman believed God. Her faith moved Jesus to respond on her behalf. Luke 8:48 states, *"Then he said to her, "Daughter, your faith has healed you. Go in peace"* (TNIV).

Are you willing to press into the Kingdom of God for your blessings? Will you commit to the journey? I believe that when we exhibit unwavering faith in God, we can rest on His word. Don't let problems deter you from receiving God's promises. We have to be as diligent as the woman with the issue of blood. She was motivated and determined to receive her blessing. She received, and so can we. As precious women of God, we can go before His throne and make our requests known.

The purpose of this chapter was to encourage you to press your way into the things of God. Regardless of circumstances, situations, or problems, don't allow them to dissuade you from seeking what God has already promised in His word. Although the answer may not come overnight, don't get discouraged—but continue to press. God rewards those who diligently seek after Him.

The next chapter reminds us that we are precious jewels in the eyes of our Heavenly Father.

God's Precious Jewel

"See how much the Father has loved us! His love is so great that we are called God's children" (1 John 3:1, GNT).

od loves you! Ladies, can you imagine that the King of Kings and Lord of Lords really does love you? Regardless of your past, your mistakes, or your problems, you are special in the eyes of God. He loves you enough that He gave His only begotten son, Jesus Christ to die on the cross for you and me. John 3:16 says, *"For God so loved the world, that he gave his only begotten son, that whosoever believe in him should not perish, but have everlasting life"* (John 3:16, KJV).

As a Christian woman, I encourage you to embrace who you are in God. He loves us beyond measure. We are His handiwork. With all of our uniqueness, we are still precious in His eyes. He is our Heavenly Father. He is the best father that one could ever have. There are many times when I just imagine laying my head on God's breast—just resting in Him. I just feel surrounded by His awesome power and glorious presence. When I was a little girl growing up in North Carolina, I recall looking up at the sky and telling the Lord that I knew He was real. At night, I would say "Goodnight, Father." Why am I sharing this? I did not grow up with a father in the home, but God became the Father that I desperately needed in my life. I knew I was His daughter and that He loved me.

When you know who you are in God, then His will and purpose for your life will take precedence over anything else. That relationship becomes the ultimate relationship. The bible declares, *"But seek ye first the kingdom of God, and his righteousness; and all these things shall be added unto you"* (Matthew 6:33, KJV).

When we put God first, we are recognizing His sovereignty. As the sovereign Lord, He will meet our every need. He knows what we need even before we ask. Just because you currently do not have a mate, doesn't mean that God is not aware of your present status. He wants you to be content with Him. Then He will bless you with who and what you need in His timing.

As Christians, we should seek to grow and mature in the knowledge of the Lord. This will enable us to make wise decisions in every aspect of our lives. This is so important. As women sometimes we make decisions based on our biological clock. I would surmise that some women have married so that they could have children. Unfortunately, their choice in mate was probably not the best decision because they made an emotional decision. The heart can be very deceptive if we do not trust in God and ask Him for wisdom and guidance. Remember, He loves us. Let God direct your steps.

Since we all have areas in our lives that we want to improve, we can use various strategies and techniques to work on spiritual and personal development. For example, we can engage in consistent prayer, corporate bible study, retreats, personal study, etc. We can even apply techniques used in the military and business today.

As a retired military officer and a certified Green Belt in Lean Six Sigma, I was trained to use a technique called the Strength, Weakness, Opportunity, and Threat (SWOT) analysis. See Table 1 below. The analysis was conducted to help organizations evaluate their investments. For example, "Should we invest in this project?" What are the pros and cons of this business endeavor? By conducting the SWOT analysis, the organization could use the results to make their decision. Although, the SWOT analysis technique has primarily been used in business and industry assessments, I wonder what would happen if we conducted a SWOT analysis on ourselves?

For example, what are your strengths and weaknesses when it comes to spiritual and personal development? Can you identify opportunities for growth? What are some things that are threatening you from becoming what God designed you to be?

Take the time to think and pray about these questions and whatever God reveals to you, write it down. Action equals results. If you are not willing to take action, you will never see any results.

Strengths	Weaknesses	Opportunities	Threats

Table 1: Example of a SWOT Diagram

After identifying those things that are presenting challenges to your spiritual and personal growth, you need to design a plan to get you on the course to becoming the better "you." Establish your vision, goals, and objectives for your personal growth plan.

Ensure that your goals have metrics that you can successfully measure on a consistent basis. Many people use the SMART technique when designing goals. The acronym has changed over the years, but primarily means the following:

- ❖ S = Specific
- ❖ M = Measurable
- ❖ A = Attainable or Achievable
- ❖ R = Relevant or Realistic
- ❖ T = Time-bound or Timely

Whether spiritual or personal, it is essential that you develop goals so that you can have something to strive toward. Take time to write the goals down so that they are visible. For example, a goal could be: *By December 31, 2013, I will consistently read the bible daily*. Although this is a simple goal, it meets the SMART criteria.

Regardless of the plan or strategy that you use, your ultimate goal is to become the best *you* that is possible. Remember, that a personal growth plan is only as good as the initiative and energy that you invest into working the plan. As a military person, we always engaged in various plans. Therefore, I am a firm believer that the plan will work if you work it. Your return on investment with your plan will be based on what you *invest* in your plan. When you encounter obstacles, don't give up—just readjust the plan.

We are God's precious jewels. He wants us to be our best. He has given all of us talents and gifts. According to 1 Peter 4:10, *"As each one has received a special gift, employ it in serving one another as good stewards of the manifold grace of God"* (NASB). In recognizing those gifts, we need to nurture and develop those gifts.

As representatives of the Most High here on the earth, we have a responsibility. When people look at us they should be able to see Jesus. Without hesitation, we should be examples for others to want to emulate. As we do what we can to improve who we are, then God will do the rest as He prepares us to receive "that" which He has for us.

Regardless of whether we are asking God for a mate or just growing from day-to-day in Him, we have to be committed to following God's plan. Psalm 37:23 states, *"The steps of a good man are ordered by the LORD: and he delighteth in his way"* (KJV). Are you following God's plan for your life? If you desire a mate, have you made that request known to God? It might take an extended time period for the answer to materialize. However, if we delight ourselves in God, then He will in due time grant our heart's desire.

This chapter reminded us that we are God's precious jewels. He loves us more than we could ever imagine. He wants what is best for us according to His plan. We were introduced to the SWOT tool which can be used to help us identify those areas in our lives that require further personal development. We also discussed the SMART technique which is used for goal setting. As representatives of the Most High, we have a responsibility to become our best.

The next chapter will discuss what happens when we step ahead of God.

What Happens When We Step Ahead of God?

Despite knowing that God will answer our prayer in His timing, sometimes we still want to expedite the process and help God out. For some reason, we think we know best. We will listen to friends, family, and even adopt some of society's habits. For a season, we may believe that everything is working fine. However, as time progresses, we realize that we made a horrendous mistake.

Although no relationship is perfect, God is perfect. He is the master designer of everything. His plan far exceeds anything that we could ever imagine. God is looking for people who are willing to trust in Him. There have been many times in my life in which I have stepped ahead of God's plan for me. On one occasion, I prematurely accepted a job. After serving in the position for a while, I realized that this was not God's perfect plan for my life. I was anxious about the position and I really thought that God wanted me to accept the job. What I realized was that I wanted the job and did not ask God if this was the job He had for me? There is a big difference.

Sometimes, we want God to agree with our plans. We will cry, beg, and plead with God to bring the petition to pass. There are times, when God will allow His *permissive will* to be activated in our lives. Yet, had we been willing to wait on Him, then we could have reaped His *perfect will*. Unfortunately, sometimes we have to suffer through the consequences of our premature desires.

We are all familiar with the story of Abraham and Sarah who desperately wanted children. God had promised them a child. Since Abraham and Sarah were getting older, they did not think that God would fulfill the promise. They are not alone. How many times have we been waiting on something from God and wanted to throw up our hands and [begin to wave them ... like we just don't care?]

During Sarah's time, not being able to bear children was considered a curse. To minimize her pain, Sarah thought that she would be proactive. Sarah offered her servant Haggai to Abraham, who gladly accepted. Would anyone have expected Abraham to respond differently?

Haggai conceived and had a son named Ishmael. Although Abraham and Sarah believed that they were doing a good thing, they did not necessarily do the "right" thing. As history records, God did fulfill the promise to Sarah and Abraham. Sarah would later conceive and have a son who was named Isaac. According to history, many of the conflicts occurring today in the Middle East can be traced back to the discord that occurred between Ishmael and Isaac. Sometimes, there can be long, extended repercussions from stepping ahead of God.

Let's look at a more compelling example. Sometimes as women we might meet a man that for all intents and purposes we think is "Mr. Right." If he is not the one—we will try to make him the one. Despite some early warning indicators, we invoke the big *ignore sign*. We put our commonsense on hold. Even the little things that we should have recognized are ignored.

Although you would think age would cause us to respond differently, it is not necessarily true. We get caught us in emotions and make ill-advised choices. We tell our friends, that we can change him or he isn't that bad. Somehow, we even try to convince ourselves that we can buy his love with "gifts." When asked by friends about the relationship, we simple ignore them or try to cover up for his shortcomings. Sometimes we use the excuse, "Oh, he is just shy." The tragic part is that we will pretend that this relationship has been ordained by God and made in heaven. Yet, God was nowhere in the making or designing of this relationship.

Sometimes, when we step ahead of God, we invite unnecessary drama into our lives. We get so involved in the wrong relationship that we miss the right relationship. At times, we assume a motherly role versus a soul-mate role. We find ourselves going through emotional relationships that will eventually destroy our self-esteem. We are not being built up, but tore down.

Our heart becomes attached to people and things that are unhealthy for us. The bible has a lot to say about the heart. According to Jeremiah 17:9, *"The heart is more deceitful than all else and is desperately sick.*

Who can understand it?" (NASB). Therefore, you cannot rely simply on the heart for direction. It is essential that we align our lives with God's word.

When we look at the divorce rate around the country today, it is alarming. We all know people who have had multiple divorces. Although there are many reasons for the high divorce rate, I would ascertain that if we had to do it over again, we would have done things differently. We would have made better decisions. Unfortunately, the church community is not exempt. This is why this issue is important. However, since we cannot change the past, there is no need to dwell on yesterday. What we can do is share our knowledge and strive to help others make better choices in their lives.

Since God is the source of all wisdom, then we need to ensure that we consult Him in all things. If we lack wisdom, all we need to do is ask God. We may never have the wisdom of Solomon, but we will receive what we need from the Lord. So, let me ask you, "Are you stepping ahead of God, or are you waiting on Him?"

The focal point of this chapter was to remind us not to step ahead of God's plan for our lives especially when it comes to relationships. Sometimes we rely on the heart to make decisions that can eventually destroy our lives. We have to depend on God. He is the source of all wisdom.

The next chapter deals with preparation as it pertains to relationships. How prepared are you to receive what God has for you?

Are You Making Yourself Discoverable?

"Who can find a virtuous woman? For her price is far above rubies" (Proverbs 31:10, KJV).

How many times have we petitioned God and asked the question, "Lord, where is he?" After years of waiting, sometimes we simple give up. Before we do that, let's peel back the onion. What would you do if the Lord asked, *"What are you doing to make yourself discoverable?"* You may wonder, "What does this question mean?" If you desire a mate, are you ready for God's man to find you? If he walked through the door right now, would you have to change a "couple" of things to even let him in? Unfortunately, if many of us were to be honest with ourselves, we would probably find things are not as organized as we may project.

The point that we must remember as Christian women is that God knows us better than we could ever know ourselves. There is nothing hidden from Him. He knows the "uncovered" you. His spotlight sees everything. For example, God knows how we conduct ourselves when fellow Christians are not present. He even knows how we take care of our bodies, and keep our homes. Most of all, God knows if we are really ready for [His] man.

God not only loves us, but He also loves the man that He has for us. Therefore, we must ask ourselves, "Are we the virtuous women that our future mates will thank God for bringing into their lives?" If marriage is your desire, "What are you doing to prepare yourself for this awesome responsibility?" Even Esther had to prepare to meet the King.

I have a wonderful friend who waited for years for God to send her a mate. She stated that during her preparation season prior to marriage, she knew that she needed to make some changes in her life. Having been single for an extended period of time presented some challenges. For example, she was comfortable with doing things her way and making her own decisions. She was responsible for no one but herself. However, these dynamics change when one gets married. Therefore, God specifically dealt with my friend about making room in her life for her mate. If you have no room in your life for someone else, then are you really ready for marriage? When my friend began the transformation process, then God began to prepare her heart for her mate. She now had room for someone else to enter.

Are you ready for your mate? Currently, are there things in your life that would prevent God from sending you that special someone? Table 2 below contains a list of questions that I invite you to review.

Questions	Comments
1. How is your relationship with God? Are you complete in Him? No man can take the place of God in your life. He can only augment but not replace.	

2. Do you truly desire to have a mate? Remember, a double-minded person is unstable in all of [her] ways. Have you made your request known to God?	
3. Are you ready to meet God's mate for you?	
4. What are you doing to prepare? If you were the *man*, would you be satisfied with you?	
5. Are you the woman of excellence that God's man would be proud to introduce as his help-mate?	
6. Are you allowing the Holy Spirit to let you know if this man is truly the one? Would you be proud to have him as the head of your household?	
7. How much do you know about this man?	

Is he a Christian? Is he in a position to have a help-mate or family? Does he have a job or means to provide for a family? Does he even want to be married?	
8. Do you have common goals and interests?	
9. Is the guy pursuing you or are you pursuing him?	
10. Are the two of you compatible?	

Table 2: Are You Ready For a Mate?

By answering these questions, you should have a better understanding of where you are in the preparation phase. Ask the Holy Spirit to guide you in answering these questions. Be open and honest with yourself. In the end, God knows if you are ready. His delay may mean that there is still work that needs to occur in you and him. Don't give up just commit to becoming the woman that God ordained you to become.

The purpose of this chapter was to challenge you to think about how prepared you are to receive God's man into your life. Despite the fact that we declare that we are ready to receive from God, sometimes we are not as prepared as we profess.

As indicated in this chapter, there are a series of questions that you can answer that will enable you to evaluate your current state. God knows your heart and "you." There is nothing hidden from the Master.

The next chapter will present some final thoughts on this topic.

Conclusions

God is involved with every aspect of our lives even to include relationships. The ultimate relationship that we want to build is our relationship with our Heavenly Father. As we nurture this relationship, God will sustain and keep us in His loving care. He is the one that we want to please. No earthly relationship can ever take the place of our relationship with our loving Father. Yet, as we delight in our Father, God will give us the desires of our heart. The bible states in Psalm 37:4, *"Take delight in the Lord and he will give you the desires of your heart"* (TNIV).

Based on God's plan for relationships, if you desire a mate, let the one that God has selected pursue you. Many times we think we know better than God. However, as women of God, let's pray first, listen closely, and remain still. Don't try to get ahead of God, but let God's timing set the stage for how you proceed forward. As was discussed in this book, we can trust God for the decision. His answer may not come when we want it, but we can rest in knowing that He has not forgotten about us.

We also looked at several questions that will challenge us to determine where we are in the preparation stage. These questions should stimulate intense discussion as you examine where you are spiritually, mentally and physically in this process. It is important that you take time to answer each of the questions before you declare that you are ready for a mate.

Based on discussions presented in this book, we also know that some people enter into ill-advised relationships. The consequences can be devastating. However, if we wait on God, we can potentially prevent unnecessary drama and heart-ache.

The premise throughout the book was that Christian women should not engage in pursuing or chasing after any man. Regardless of what society may postulate as acceptable social practices, God's word is our guidepost and standard. We are His representatives on the earth. People should see a difference in our lives. Although the world advocates that it is okay for women to pursue men that is not God's pattern for relationships. Unfortunately, as we saw in the informal survey that was conducted with 100 participants, 70% of the respondents indicated that it is acceptable for women to pursue men.

As I conclude this book, my prayer is that these words will bless your life, and that you will continue to strive to be God's Woman of Excellence. I pray that He will use you to be a blessing to others. If you truly desire to be married, in His timing, God will present you to the one that He has chosen for you. Take courage and be confident that God's way is truly the best way.

Be blessed and know that He is God!

Appendix A

This appendix provides space for you to spend time in silent reflection. After having read this book, I want you to take time to write down the life lessons that will enable you to grow in God.

_____

_____

_____

_____

_____

_____

_____

Appendix B

This appendix provides an opportunity for you to identify spiritual and personal goals that you would like to accomplish over the next year.

1._____

2._____

3._____

4._____

5._____

6._____

Appendix C

This appendix provides an opportunity for you to identify your **strengths**. What are your God-given gifts? Can you maximize those strengths in your life?

1._____

2._____

3._____

4._____

5._____

6._____

Appendix D

This appendix provides an opportunity for you to identify **weaknesses** that you would like to improve. It is not until we identify those areas, that we can actually begin to improve those areas.

1._____

2._____

3._____

4._____

5._____

6._____

Appendix E

This appendix provides an area for you to identify **opportunities** that will enable you to grow both spiritually and professionally.

1._____

2._____

3._____

4._____

5._____

6._____

Appendix F

This appendix provides an opportunity for you to identify those things that could **threaten** or prevent you from becoming the best that God designed you to be. For example, one can choose to settle for "not being good enough, when God has already designed you for greatness." Are your thoughts threatening your progress?

1._____

2._____

3._____

4._____

5._____

6._____

About the Author

Dr. Mary M. Gillam is a business owner, poet, motivational speaker, and retired Air Force Colonel with over 28 years of military service. After retiring from the military, Dr. Gillam worked as a government contractor for Booz Allen Hamilton. She was later appointed to the Senior Executive Service (SES) at the Office of the Secretary of Defense in the Pentagon where she served as the Director of Technology, Innovation and Engineering. After experiencing the entrepreneur bug, she decided to start her own company.

Dr. Gillam is currently the president and owner of M²G Dynamic Leadership Solutions, and the Mary M. Gillam Literary Enterprise, LLC. Both companies are service disabled veteran owned businesses.

A native of Roseboro, North Carolina, Dr. Gillam was raised by her paternal grandmother under very humble conditions. Her first book, "*I Never Said Good-bye*" was a special tribute to her grandmother who passed while she was stationed in Korea. The book is also a testament of Dr. Gillam's strong faith. Dr. Gillam is also the author of, "*A Jewel Collage of Poetry.*"

Having spent over 30 years working in information systems, Dr. Gillam is the author of, "*Information Warfare: Combating the Threat in the 21st Century,*" and "*Exploring the Impact of the Clinger-Cohen Act of 1996 on Information Technology Governance.*" A seasoned executive and servant-leader, Dr. Gillam is currently working on another book entitled, "*The CORE Leadership Development Model: 4 Steps to Releasing Your Leadership Potential.*"

Dr. Gillam has a Bachelor of Science degree in Chemistry from North Carolina A&T State University, three Masters Degrees to include a Masters in Computers and Information Resource Management from Webster University. She also has a Graduate Certificate in Legislative Studies from Georgetown University, a Graduate Certificate in Project Management from Villanova, and a Doctorate in Management Information Systems Technology from the University of Phoenix. Dr. Gillam is a graduate of the military's Naval War College in Newport, RI, and the Air Command & Staff College in Montgomery, AL. She has been awarded multiple military and leadership awards to include the Spirit of the American Woman Leadership Award and the Federal Women's Executive Leadership Award. She also has a Green Belt in Lean Six Sigma.

Most importantly, Dr. Gillam is a born-again Christian. Having been called to Evangelism in September 1990, Dr. Gillam is currently enrolled in the Religious Education doctoral program at International Seminary in Florida.